Original title:
Ripe with Hope

Copyright © 2025 Creative Arts Management OÜ
All rights reserved.

Author: Colin Harrington
ISBN HARDBACK: 978-1-80586-300-7
ISBN PAPERBACK: 978-1-80586-772-2

Fields of Unseen Possibilities

In fields where dreams are slightly bent,
The grass has laughter, nature's scent.
A squirrel juggles with acorn flair,
While daisies whisper, 'Life's unfair.'

The clouds wear hats, quite out of style,
As ants parade, they march a mile.
With wild ideas growing like weeds,
We plant our quips, and watch it breed.

Bounty of Belief

There's treasure in the cereal bowl,
Where marshmallows bubble, heart and soul.
My spoon's a shovel, digging deep,
In this frosty castle, dreams don't sleep.

Goldfish swim in a lemonade sea,
Their scales shimmer wildly, carelessly free.
With giggles bursting, like popcorn's cheer,
A feast for the soul, come grab a beer!

A Garden of Dreams Awaits

In gardens where the giggles bloom,
We plant our jokes amidst the gloom.
Gnomes are grinning, their shine so bright,
As flowers pop in a silly fight.

Butterflies wear socks, what a sight!
They flutter past in pure delight.
With every bloom, a chuckle shared,
In our secret garden, nothing's spared.

The Sunlit Path Ahead

The sunbeams dance like silly sprites,
Leading us down to wondrous heights.
We stumble and trip on laughter's tune,
While shadows giggle beneath the moon.

With every step, a chuckle rolls,
As daisies tumble, they're on their strolls.
Let's skip along this comical way,
Tomorrow comes, so let's play today!

In the Shadow of Sunshine

The sun shines bright, my hat flies high,
Chasing dreams, I stumble, oh my!
A bird steals fries, it's quite the show,
Laughter erupts, as time slips slow.

The ice cream melts, my hands a mess,
Life's little quirks, I must confess,
In each goofy dance, joy blooms anew,
Under sunshine's gaze, the world feels true.

Tides of Bright Futures

Waves of wishes crash on the shore,
My boat's a toy, what's in store?
Seagulls chat gossip, oh what a scene,
The future waves back, "What do you mean?"

With each dip and splash, laughter's found,
Even fish seem to wiggle around.
In this playful sea, I'll cast my net,
For dreams that tickle and never fret.

Cherished Aspirations

In the garden of hopes, a cat lays fat,
Dreams bloom like daisies, imagine that!
With every sneeze, new plans arise,
Water them well, laughter is wise.

Planting giggles, they sprout and play,
Chasing squirrels, they dance away.
Each step I take toward aspirations bright,
Frolicking fun, oh what a sight!

The Light That Awaits

Under a streetlamp, shadows do waltz,
I trip on my shoelace, oh what a fault!
Yet, in the glow, my giggles ignite,
Chasing small wishes, a comical sight.

Streetlights giggle, they flicker and beam,
In the glimmer, I dare to dream.
Bright paths ahead, adventures unfold,
Filled with laughter, and stories retold.

The Glow of New Beginnings

In the garden where dreams sprout,
Silly seeds dance about.
They giggle and they twirl,
Wishing for a twinkling pearl.

Butterflies chuckle in the breeze,
As flowers play tricks with the bees.
Sunshine tickles the green lawn,
Laughter echoes from dusk till dawn.

Tiny sprouts wear their best hats,
Playing games with the gossiping cats.
Every leaf is a happy grin,
Each bud a chance to chuckle and spin.

So here's to the fun we find,
In fresh starts and a curious mind.
With every bloom, a silly cheer,
New adventures await us here.

Ebb and Flow of Hope

Like waves that splash with delight,
Dreams bobbing, oh what a sight!
Sometimes they crash, other times they glide,
But they never flee, always abide.

A jellyfish floats, full of schemes,
While seahorses dive into their dreams.
Coral reefs whisper silly tales,
Of shimmering fish with glittering scales.

The tide rolls in, takes worries away,
With laughter and joy, come what may.
Sandcastles rise, sometimes they fall,
Yet we build them again, standing tall.

So laugh with the ocean's playful tune,
As the sun plays peek-a-boo with the moon.
Each swell brings a chuckle and glee,
In this dance of life, so wild and free.

Petals Under the Sun

Daisies get together for a ball,
Wearing goofy hats, standing tall.
Daffodils dance, prancing about,
Swapping stories, having a shout.

Tulips giggle with a cheeky grin,
While roses puff like they've got kin.
The sun sets a stage, so bright and bold,
For petals to shine, and laughter to hold.

A bumblebee brings a tune to sing,
While ladybugs join in on the swing.
They twirl under rays, each shines so bright,
In this ridiculous garden of delight.

So here's to petals, to laughter and cheer,
To growing together, year after year.
With every bloom, bright colors appear,
Making the world seem much more clear.

Journey to the Horizon

With backpacks stuffed full of dreams,
We set off with silly beams.
Maps that tickle and giggle a lot,
Leading us towards the next silly plot.

We ride on clouds, floating real high,
As we wave to the stars passing by.
The sun is a grin, the moon just winks,
With every giggle, our spirit drinks.

From mountains tall to rivers wide,
Adventure awaits on this joyful ride.
Each step we take, we laugh and cheer,
Finding joy in each moment we steer.

So off we go, seeking fun untold,
With a pinch of laughter, and hearts bold.
Our journey's just starting, the horizon glows,
With every giggle, our excitement grows.

The Bloom of Tomorrow

In the garden where daisies dance,
Dandelions sing, oh what a chance!
Bumblebees buzzing without a care,
Even the weeds are trying to share.

Sunflowers grinning at passersby,
Waving their petals, oh so spry!
Plant a joke, water it with cheer,
Watch giggles bloom through every sphere.

Kayaks of Dreams

In a sea of thoughts afloat,
Paddling wild in a tiny boat.
Fish wear hats, and seagulls squawk,
Dreams ride waves, come take a walk!

Alligators making a splash,
Telling tales of their goldfish stash.
With laughter as my trusty guide,
I'll paddle on with irony wide.

Under the Canopy of Promise

Trees are gossiping, branches sway,
Leaves drop hints, come out to play.
Under twinkling lights they hum,
Secrets shared, oh, what's to come?

Squirrels debating on which tree's best,
Chasing dreams, a feathery jest.
Mushrooms giggling in the dark,
Night whispers tales that leave a mark.

Paths Yet Untrodden

Footsteps dance on paths unknown,
Adventures waiting, seeds are sown.
A path of rubber ducks ahead,
Where silly creatures dare to tread.

Maps drawn by a toddler's hand,
Leading us to the jellybean land.
With sock puppets as our guides,
We'll run and laugh, oh how it glides!

Colors of Anticipation

A rainbow sprinkles dreams on ice,
Gummy bears dance, oh what a slice.
We spin in circles, joy's parade,
In bubblegum clouds, our plans are made.

Pineapple hats upon our heads,
Jellybean shoes, wherever we tread.
Lemonade rivers, we float and sing,
With sparkly gummy worms as our bling.

Expectations hop like frogs in a pot,
While chocolate bunnies share their plot.
We chuckle and smile, the future's bright,
With whipped cream clouds in the morning light.

So gather 'round, let the colors play,
In this silly scheme, we'll find our way.
With each giggle, a new path appears,
In a world made of laughter, we'll crush our fears.

The Fruit of Our Endeavors

Bananas in pajamas conquer the day,
Wobbling like jelly, they dance and sway.
Mangoes giggle, just off the tree,
As oranges plot their escape with glee.

Weaving ideas like a spider's web,
From mischief to magic, we each ebb.
Strawberry dreams on a buttery toast,
Let's toast to the fruit that we love the most.

Winners and losers, we all take a chance,
Cabbage in tutus, they join the dance.
With every bite, a giggle arises,
As we savor the tart and sweet surprises.

So plant your seeds in this fun-filled ground,
Where laughter and fruity joys abound.
For every endeavor, we munch and we crunch,
In this garden of dreams, let's all have a bunch!

Whispers of a New Beginning

The dawn brings giggles, fresh and bright,
Chickens cluck jokes, what a delight!
Butterflies bounce on a trampoline sky,
As we spread our wings, ready to fly.

Morning glories laugh at the sun,
With each dew drop, it's all in good fun.
Silly squirrels plot their wild schemes,
In the land of curious, where all is dreams.

New paths unfurl like silly string,
Each twist and turn invites us to sing.
With lollipop clouds, we skip through the air,
A symphony of chuckles, beyond compare.

So gather your joy, set it free,
In this whimsical dance, just you and me.
For every whisper, a chance to delight,
With silly beginnings, we'll soar to new height.

Echoes of Resilience

Bounce back like a rubber chicken's flaps,
Life's lessons come with giggles and claps.
Wobbling through troubles like jello on a plate,
We laugh at our stumbles, and celebrate fate.

Like the sunflowers grinning, tall and proud,
We shake off the rain, join the crowd.
With cupcakes and sprinkles, we weather all storms,
In this circus of life, we find our true forms.

Each challenge a puzzle, we twist and we turn,
Finding joy in the lessons, each time we learn.
With silly hats and polka-dot shoes,
We dance through the echoes, with nothing to lose.

So raise your glass of giggles to cheer,
For resilience is sweet, and we have no fear.
In this carnival of laughter, let's take our stance,
With echoes of joy, let's join the dance!

Threads of Light

In a world of tangled twine,
We weave our dreams just fine.
With colors bright and laughter loud,
We'll fashion a blanket for the crowd.

Frogs dance with spoons in hand,
While ducks debate their breakfast plan.
Each stitch a spark of silly cheer,
With every thread, we draw love near.

So let the needles fly about,
And let no frowns be in the rout.
For joy is found in every seam,
And life's a whimsical, joyous dream.

A New Dawn Rising

As the sun peeks through the blinds,
A rooster sings, but no one minds.
The toast pops up with a little dance,
And coffee cups await their chance.

With cats in suits, and dogs in ties,
We shuffle 'round with sleepy eyes.
But with each yawning stretch we take,
The giggles rise, our hearts awake.

The world's a stage, the morning bright,
All creatures ready for the fight.
Today's the day we'll laugh and play,
Tomorrow? Well, that's just cliché.

Wave the Flag of Tomorrow

With a funny flag, we'll take a stand,
Galloping through life, hand in hand.
Bluebirds chirp like off-key notes,
While squirrels practice their silly quotes.

Tomorrow's banner flying high,
Recycles dreams like a pizza pie.
We'll conquer fears with every cheer,
And celebrate all that's truly dear.

So toss confetti, shout hooray,
Life's a circus, come what may.
With every twist and every turn,
Our laughs will light the world's great fern.

On the Edge of the Horizon

Standing where the sky meets sea,
With jellybeans as a VIP.
We dance like fish, we jump like frogs,
And sing with gusto 'til the sun logs.

The edge is bright, it sparkles true,
Like sparkly shoes in a muddy pool.
So let's toast marshmallows on this ride,
With chocolate dreams we'll never hide.

We'll paint our futures with silly sighs,
And wear our hopes like butterfly ties.
For every moment holds a song,
Join the fun, you can't go wrong!

Dreams Growing on the Vine

In the garden, dreams do stretch,
Each one bright, a little sketch.
A cucumber jokes, and a pumpkin sings,
Telling tales of silly things.

The tomatoes giggle, red and round,
Whispers of laughter in the ground.
With sunlit smiles, they twirl and dance,
Inviting all to join the prance.

Carrots wearing glasses, oh what a sight,
Debating wisdom with all their might.
Beneath the leaves, the radishes cheer,
In this quirky patch, there's nothing to fear.

So let's toast to vines, both tall and low,
For dreams are silly seeds that grow.
In laughter's light, we plant our cheer,
Harvesting joy, year after year.

Sunrise on the Edge of Tomorrow

The sun peeks up, a golden grin,
Waking the world with a silly spin.
A rooster crows, sporting a tie,
Announcing the day with a feathery sigh.

Clouds fluff up like cotton candy,
While squirrels make plans that are quite handy.
With bouncing beans, they leap and play,
Chasing shadows till the end of the day.

The horizon's edge, a dance of light,
Promises mischief, morning delight.
With breakfast dreams on toasty plates,
We share a giggle, and it resonates.

So here's to sunrises, bright and bold,
With tales of fun waiting to unfold.
We'll toast to laughter as day begins,
On the edge of tomorrow, where hope always wins.

Harvest of Dreams

The harvest moon, a playful sight,
Dances with stars in the cool, crisp night.
Pumpkins in line for a dance-off spree,
While corn's taking selfies, 'Look at me!'

Underneath moons so full and bright,
Inspirations flutter like bugs in flight.
Each dream gathered in a basket wide,
With giggles spilling from inside.

Apple trees tease with shiny red,
As whispers of dreams bounce overhead.
"Pick me! Pick me!" the cherries shout,
In this harvest, we'll laugh and sprout.

So let's gather dreams like autumn leaves,
In playful heaps, oh how it weaves!
With laughter sweet as cider's flow,
In a harvest of dreams, we'll always glow.

Blossoms of Tomorrow

Blossoms bloom with a cheeky grin,
Winking at bees buzzing, 'Come right in!'
Each petal flutters, a brilliant hue,
Creating ballet, just for a few.

In the garden of whimsy, bright and spry,
Buds take flight, like balloons up high.
They dance on stems, a festival fair,
Swaying in laughter, light as air.

Sunflowers bow with a gentle sway,
Chasing the sun and the clouds at play.
With daisies giggling, a flower parade,
In petals, the secrets of joy are laid.

So let's plant smiles, give seeds a toss,
For blossoms of cheer, we'll never lose gloss.
In the garden of laughter, dreams shall borrow,
A springtime of joy, with tomorrow's glow.

Leaves of Liberation

In a garden full of greens, they giggle,
Where tomatoes dance with a cucumber wiggle.
The carrots sport shades, oh what a sight,
While lettuce debates if it's day or night.

With radishes hatching silly plans round,
They whisper secrets from under the ground.
Peas join in with their pod-sized shoes,
Swaying and laughing like they've got nothing to lose.

Whispers of a Brighter Day

A squirrel dressed sharp, with a tiny briefcase,
Hustles acorns like he's winning a race.
Birds sing silly songs in the high, blue sky,
While clouds wear pajamas, floating by.

The sun throws rays that tickle the trees,
Making shadows dance, swaying with ease.
A caterpillar jokes, 'Life's all about speed!',
But he's just inching along—oh, the greed!

Embracing the Unfolding

Dandelions burst forth in a wild, bright spree,
With wishes afloat like giggles from a bee.
Each bud is a promise, dressed in a grin,
Saying, 'Join the fun, let the games begin!'

Butterflies flutter in a curious dance,
Flirting with flowers in a pollen-filled trance.
While bees ask for plans at the nectar café,
As they buzz about, making a joyful ballet.

A Tapestry of Dreams

In a world woven tight with colorful threads,
Where each silly dream wears its own silly head.
A race of bright kittens in hats on their paws,
Compete for the title of 'The Best Joke Draws!'

Jellybeans giggle as rain turns to sprinkles,
While cupcakes plan parties with zany winks and crinkles.
Under a moon that chuckles and sways,
They celebrate laughter in the most whimsical ways.

Harmony in Hues

Colors collide in a silly dance,
Like a cat that thinks it can prance.
Brushes chuckle, paint spills around,
As they giggle on the canvas ground.

Shades of laughter, a bright confetti,
A rainbow skims, oh so petty.
Each hue whispers, 'Join the spree!'
With a wink, they claim, 'Just be free!'

Splashes of orange, a cheeky trick,
Paint the town with a vibrant flick.
Let the blues sing, and yellows play,
In this joyful jam, let's sway away!

So grab your palette, don't be absurd,
Join the fun, not a single word.
For in this chaos, joy is found,
In every brushstroke, laughter's crowned.

The Call of New Frontiers

Off we go, on a wild quest,
Chasing dreams with a goofy jest.
Maps upside down, a laugh or two,
"Who needs directions when we've got a view?"

With every step, a wobbly dance,
A tumble here, a laughing glance.
Exploring worlds with a cheeky grin,
Every stumble is just a win!

Sailing seas of spaghetti strands,
With meatball islands, oh so grand.
Pirate parrots squawk with glee,
Saying, "Adventurers, come sail with me!"

To new frontiers, we tip our hats,
Riding llamas, and befriending cats.
In the land of giggles, we shall roam,
For laughter is the greatest home.

A Dawn Yet Unwritten

Morning chirps with a silly tune,
As coffee spills—oops, there goes the spoon!
Sunshine tickles the sleepy eyes,
A dance of shadows 'neath brightening skies.

Time to play with the day ahead,
Writing tales that dance instead.
To turn mundane into something grand,
With doodles and giggles, let's take a stand!

Expect the unexpected, they say,
As toast pops up, in a funny way.
Butterflies waltz on the morning breeze,
While socks parade like they own the trees.

In this dawn yet to unfold,
Each moment's a gem that glimmers bold.
So grab your joy and give a shout,
For the day's unwritten—let's check it out!

Flourishing Futures

In gardens where the daisies dance,
The future wears a funny stance,
With squirrels plotting in the trees,
And bees that buzz in rhymes with ease.

The carrots joke about their height,
While radishes put up a fight,
A pumpkin wearing a top hat wide,
Shrieks laughter as it rolls with pride.

The sun's a comedian up above,
Telling clouds to lighten up and shove,
While rainbows giggle in the sky,
Playing hide and seek as they fly.

In kitchens, pots begin to sing,
Mixing joy in everything,
Flour and sugar do a jig,
While cake pops up, all bright and big.

Threads of Tomorrow

Knitting dreams with yarn so bright,
The future's wrapped in pure delight,
With every stitch a silly grin,
And laughter woven deep within.

The needles tap a merry beat,
As visions dance on nimble feet,
While patterns form in zigzag ways,
Each knot a charm for sunny days.

The tapestry of life displayed,
With colors bold, they've got it made,
A cat that sneezes, yarn on spree,
Making sure we giggle, whee!

In every twist, a joke unfolds,
A tale of whimsy yet untold,
So grab a thread, come join the fun,
Tomorrow's bright, let's start to run!

Unfolding Potential

Like origami in the breeze,
With paper cranes doing as they please,
A swan might quack, a frog could leap,
As secrets of the world we keep.

Each fold reveals a quirky twist,
In shapes and forms that can't be missed,
A fortune cookie's wise old line,
Proclaims that humor's truly divine.

The future's crafting out of sight,
With giggles hanging in the light,
As paper hats on heads do sway,
Making every moment a play.

With colors vivid and hearts so bold,
Each laugh a gem, a sight to behold,
So watch as dreams begin to sprout,
In ways that make us laugh and shout!

When Stars Align

The stars are juggling in the night,
Tossing wishes with delight,
While comets race, they spin and play,
Whispering secrets as they sway.

A moonbeam winks at passing ships,
While galaxies perform their flips,
Shooting stars take daring dives,
Knitting magic in our lives.

The universe holds a cosmic grin,
As surprises dance and twist within,
Planets laugh in an endless chase,
Inviting all to join the space.

So when you gaze at that night sky,
Know there's fun beneath that pie,
For joy erupts when stars align,
In a universe that's ours to shine!

Notes of a Brighter Day

The sun peeked out, a wink so bright,
A squirrel danced, a silly sight.
Birds began to sing their tune,
While flowers giggled, chasing the moon.

A joke was told by winds that blew,
As butterflies wore hats, all askew.
The daisies rolled in laughter's fray,
Chasing clouds in a lighthearted play.

Lemonade stands sprouted like trees,
With giggles shared in a warm breeze.
The world spun 'round in a jolly mess,
As joy unraveled in pure, sweet excess.

So here's to the cheer that bounces along,
In the garden where the happy belong.
With every chuckle, the day's parade,
In a symphony of smiles, our dreams are made.

A Garden of Possibilities

In a patch of sun where carrots wave,
Tomatoes giggled, oh how they behave!
Radishes wore shades, feeling quite cool,
While peas popped jokes, breaking all the rules.

The garden gnomes are up to no good,
Plotting pranks in their leafy wood.
Bees buzzed by with tales of delight,
As marigolds spun in a flower fight.

With cucumbers dressed in polka dot pants,
They laughed at the squash, in silly dance.
Sunflowers tangled in taffy threads,
Whispering secrets, rolling their heads.

So plant a seed of joy today,
Where laughter blooms in an endless way.
In this garden where giggles grow,
The sunshine's glow makes our spirits overflow.

Beyond the Gloom

When shadows linger, and sighs are near,
A penguin slips on ice, oh dear!
Raindrops tap-dance on windowpanes,
While laughter breaks the dullest chains.

A naughty breeze steals your hat away,
As giggles bounce like a game of play.
Clouds float by, wearing frowns upside down,
And the moon tickles stars in a shimmering gown.

Gremlins of gloom tuck their tails in shame,
As humor takes charge of the silly game.
With each little chuckle, the shadows retreat,
Inviting the sun to join in the feat.

So take a step into the light's embrace,
Where fun takes over, and problems erase.
Beyond the gloom lies a playful spree,
In the laughter's rhythm, we're wild and free!

Luminous Visions

In a world where colors sing and sway,
A dancing jellybean leads the way.
With sparkly shoes on its wobbly feet,
It twirls through laughter and sugary sweet.

Rainbows paint mischief in the sky,
While gummy bears bounce and fly high.
Pineapples wear crowns that shimmer bright,
As laughter explodes in pure, fizzy delight.

Each bubble formed is a wish come true,
As whimsy and giggles come rushing through.
Chasing shadows with a playful grin,
In this circus of joy, let the fun begin!

With luminous visions in every gaze,
We dance through nonsense, in carefree phase.
So let's celebrate with giggles galore,
In our world of wonder, forever we soar!

A Canvas Brushed with Light

In a world where lemons dance bright,
Painted smiles on a canvas, oh what a sight.
Jellybeans laughing, bubblegum dreams,
Cheerful whispers float on chocolate streams.

Puddles giggle, as they splash with glee,
Sunshine tickles the grass, can you see?
Cotton candy clouds drift, making us grin,
The laughter of colors, where joy begins.

A rainbow of mischief up high in the sky,
Where playful thoughts wiggle and hop, oh my!
Each brushstroke a secret, a chuckle, a cheer,
With every hue, a chance to steer clear.

So let's color our worries with hues of delight,
In a world of pure whimsy, let's take flight.
Painting our days with a wink and a nod,
Life's a funny canvas—and we are its god!

Potential Unfurled

From tiny seeds sprouting, a dance in the dust,
They wiggle and giggle, oh what a must!
With twirling leaves, they burst out in cheer,
Ants tell jokes as they gather near.

Each blossom a grin tilting out of the ground,
Nature's hoedown, where joy is unbound.
With petals all prepped, they par-tay in the sun,
Take that, Mr. Gloom, we're having some fun!

Bumblebees buzzing, with hats of fine style,
Dancing in circles, it's quite the guile.
They sip on sweet nectar, their tiny wee cups,
Turning fears into laughter, oh, what a mix-up!

Life sprouts in odd places, like mushrooms on logs,
Turning mundane moments into jolly little frogs.
So let's stretch our limbs, let our worries unfurl,
And embrace the absurd in this wacky, wild whirl!

Threads of Radiance Woven

In a tapestry bright, woven with flair,
Each thread a story, wrapped with some care.
Frogs in top hats play chess on the lawn,
As the moon whispers secrets till the break of dawn.

Stray cats in tutus prance by with delight,
Poking fun at shadows, what a silly sight!
While stars twinkle giggles in the velvety sea,
Creating new patterns, just you wait and see.

Yarns of hoot owls that wink in the night,
Perched above chortling, oh what a sight!
They weave funny tales on their looms of bright dreams,
Cross-stitching giggles like wild, vibrant streams.

So come spin a yarn with the weavers of smiles,
In a world filled with laughter, let's gather in piles!
For every thread tangled, brings joy to the fold,
In this fabric of funny, let the stories unfold!

The Promise of New Valleys

In valleys of whimsy, where giggles abound,
Lollipops sprout from the soft, cuddly ground.
Marshmallow hills rise up, fluffy and wide,
With gummy bears waiting to join in the ride.

The squirrels play tag with the sun on their tail,
While wise old turtles regale us with tales.
Twinkling flowers do a waltz in the breeze,
Sharing funny jokes with the buzzing dear bees.

Each sunrise a chuckle, bursting with cheer,
Bananas in pajamas sing songs we hold dear.
The path might be silly and covered in fluff,
But in these new valleys, there's more than enough.

So let's frolic in joy, with brightness to spare,
In the playground of life, where no frown can bear.
Revel in the echoes of laughter's sweet call,
For in every new valley, there's magic for all!

Starry Paths Ahead

With shoes untied and socks that clash,
We dance through puddles, making a splash.
The stars up high wink down at me,
As if to say, "Look, you're fancy and free!"

We trip on poodles, chase a stray cat,
Life's little details, where's the mat?
The sky's a canvas, we'll paint it bright,
With goofy grins, we'll own the night!

A Tapestry of Promise

Grandma's knitting brings forth delight,
Her yarn sings songs of playful fright.
Every stitch holds a tale of cheer,
Of socks gone rogue and cakes that veer!

A patchwork quilt, where giggles blend,
Unraveling stories we can't comprehend.
Tangled threads, but oh, what fun,
We'll knot our lives 'til the day is done!

The Warmth of Grass Beneath

Rolling around on a sunlit field,
With ants on our legs, our laughter's revealed.
We roast the sun, but never burn,
While whispers of summer in breezes churn.

A picnic planned, but ants just feast,
Our lunch transformed to an insect feast.
Grass stains on knees, oh what a fright,
But hey, it's a party, and we own the night!

The Dawn of Dreams

Morning light creeps, with a wink and a nud,
Floating away like a fluffy green bud.
With toast that's burned and jelly askew,
We launch our day with a giggly brew.

Tickled by breezes that dance through our hair,
Morning giggles float, without a care.
So grab your dreams, toss your woes,
In fields of laughter where happiness grows!

Seeds of Change

A garden of dreams, where ducks wear hats,
Sunflowers dance and chat with the cats.
Gnomes tell jokes, they bubble with cheer,
Worms hold a banquet, oh what a year!

Frogs leap for joy in polka-dot shoes,
Mice in tuxedos sip sweet lemonade brews.
Every seed sown feels like a joke,
As flowers burst forth, the soil they poke.

With trowels a-clattering, we plant some delight,
Sunbathing daisies share laughs in the light.
Breezes carry giggles, oh such a spree,
In this wacky patch, we chuckle with glee.

And though weeds may peek with mischief and flair,
We tickle the roots with a comical scare.
For laughter's the key to this sprightly dance,
As sprouts wiggle wearin' a silly romance.

Radiance in Shadow

In the corners where sunlight dares not tread,
A cactus wears glasses as it reads in bed.
The shadows are filled with a whimsical tune,
As bats hold a concert beneath the full moon.

Fairies in capes fly and giggle with glee,
While sleeping gnomes dream of a bumblebee spree.
Mushrooms wear hats, with style so divine,
They dance on tiptoes with a glass of sweet wine.

Smoky laughs linger, like clouds made of fluff,
As owls in tuxedos discuss their own stuff.
The glowworms throw parties for folks passing through,
Illuminating mischief, oh what a view!

In twilight's embrace, the puns never cease,
With shadows for allies, the laughter's increased.
Each crack in the dark shines bright with a jest,
So come join the mirth; it's simply the best!

A New Leaf Turns

A book of bright leaves flips over with flair,
Each page a giggle in sunny, warm air.
Squirrels in sneakers basketball on high,
While tulips throw shade with a flower-power sigh.

Blowing dandelions send wishes afloat,
Each puff a chuckle, nothing to gloat.
The vines start to twist like they know the beat,
While gravelly stones hold a tap-dance retreat.

Bumblebees waltz with their pollen-filled sacks,
Crickets perform on their tiny green tracks.
A leaf flutters down, like a wink from above,
And all of the branches embrace it with love.

So let's tiptoe softly, the joy we'll discern,
In this quirky garden, a new leaf will turn.
With nature laughing, what more could we need?
In this comical realm, hope's planted as seed!

The Echo of New Beginnings

In the land of the chuckles where funny things grow,
Echoes of laughter create a grand show.
The sun tickles blades of grass with a tease,
While butterflies giggle and float on the breeze.

Each dawn brings a joke, a new line to share,
With socks on the line waving like they care.
Chirping with joy, the robins compose,
An anthem of mischief in rows, oh what prose!

The path to tomorrow is lined with delight,
Where hedgehogs do yoga in morning's first light.
Every bud opens to sing a small song,
As blossoms erupt in a whiff of what's wrong.

And when night falls down, the stars start to giggle,
As fireflies waltz through the trees, oh so little.
With each laugh resounding, the universe hints,
That new beginnings are where humor prints!

Whispering Willows of Change

Willows whisper scandalous tales,
Of the squirrels who wear cute veils.
They chat about dreams high in the air,
Hoping the bees will swoon in despair.

The frogs wear tuxes at the grand ball,
While crickets recite Shakespeare, brave and tall.
The owls hoot jokes, they think they're slick,
As the rain dances by, with a comic flick.

The wind fumbles while doing the cha-cha,
Trees laugh at everyone, 'Ain't this a saga?'
Each leaf is a grin, twirling in glee,
Nature's a stand-up, don't you agree?

So come join the fun, it's quite a show,
Where laughter and whimsy continuously flow.
Change is a jester, here to amuse,
In this forest of joy, you can't refuse.

The Color of Hope

In a world filled with bright polka dots,
The penguins have taken up knitting pots.
They'll weave the sun into scarves of gold,
As they trade silly stories, never too old.

Robins paint their beaks with rainbow hues,
While the bunnies compete for the best snooze.
They hop with flair, twirling with delight,
Under the stars that twinkle at night.

The daisies wear shades, so chic and bold,
While butterflies giggle, legends unfolded.
Pineapples wearing hats promote cheer,
In this colorful world, everyone's near.

So grab your brush, let's color a dream,
With laughter and joy, nothing's as it seems.
Together we'll paint the skies all aglow,
In this vivid parade, let cheer overflow!

Petals in the Stream

Petals float by, all pink and sweet,
With turtles reciting poetry, oh what a feat!
They trade snide comments about passing leaves,
While frogs throw confetti, giggling in eaves.

A salmon plays guitar, it's quite the show,
The kingfisher dances, stealing the flow.
As ducks form a conga line through the bramble,
The river erupts with giggles—just a ramble.

Sunlight winks down, a mischievous tease,
While otters juggle shells with delicate ease.
Each ripple's a joke, each splash a pun,
In this wild party, the fun's never done!

So come on downstream, let worries all part,
In a world made of whispers, let's all take heart.
Where petals keep dancing, the stream flows in tune,
With laughter like music, beneath the bright moon.

Built From Dreams

In a world built of marshmallows and cream,
The clouds host a concert, wind's the dream team.
Elephants tap-dance in oversized shoes,
While kittens serve popcorn, oh what a ruse!

The stars wear top hats, twinkling in glee,
While rabbits in tuxes sip tea by the sea.
Every giggle's a note, the joy's so profound,
As imagination soars, it knows no bound.

With castles of jelly, a fun-filled embrace,
Every corner's a smile, every turn's a grace.
The laughter's contagious, like bubbles in air,
Building a world that's beyond compare!

So let's join the fun, where dreams come alive,
With candy-floss wishes, together we thrive.
In this curious realm, let happiness beam,
Where life's an adventure, built from a dream!

Vows of Spring's Awakening

Tiny blooms pop up with glee,
Even trees are cracking jokes, you see!
The squirrels dance in their fluffy suits,
Chasing bees in bootless boots.

The sun spills laughter on the grass,
While frogs in leaps try to surpass.
Buds show off their pastel hues,
And even bunnies sing the blues!

Puddles laugh when puddle-jumpers arrive,
A splashy show, oh how they thrive!
Dandelion fluff joins the fray,
Spreading giggles along the way.

So here's to spring, a merry sight,
With whimsy waking day and night.
Each petal grins, each twirl's a chance,
In nature's playful, joyful dance.

Sowing Seeds of Change

Gardeners plot with a cheeky grin,
Digging up dirt, let the fun begin!
Seeds of laughter scattered here and there,
With every sprout, a reason to share.

The daisies gossip, the lilies laugh,
While tomatoes throw a water splash bath.
Planting tales that tickle the roots,
Growing in giggles, sprouting in suits!

We plant our dreams in spades of good cheer,
Worms wiggle close, they're the life of the year.
With laughter's sunlight and soil's embrace,
We'll sprout some mischief, put smiles in place!

So tend to your garden, have a ball,
For change will dance in the laughter of all.
With each seed sown, a chuckle unfurls,
In the zany world of floral swirls.

Eager Buds Awaiting Growth

Buds peek out with hopeful faces,
Like kids sneaking treats from hidden places.
They shiver with excitement in the breeze,
Ready to grow like they're professionals at tease!

Their colors blush, they shake and shiver,
While critters nearby whisper and quiver.
Bees audition for a buzzing show,
As blossoms giggle, "Look at us grow!"

Each petal winks, each stem has flair,
Who knew that blooms could style their hair?
The garden's runway, a fashion spree,
Where flowers bloom with pure esprit!

So let's cheer for each budding flower,
For funny stems with a penchant for power.
They'll strut their stuff as the sun beams bright,
In the quirky show of nature's delight.

Wings of Intent Beneath the Sky

Butterflies plot their skyward flight,
With dreams like candy, all sugary bright.
They flap their wings in a raucous game,
Like little pilots without any shame!

Clouds pass by, laughing in white,
As birds do flips, oh what a sight!
Aerial acrobats in a breeze so fine,
Chasing jokes in a playful line.

The sun whispers secrets to the night,
While stars dance like they're ready to fight.
Even the moon grins wide with mirth,
Under skies full of playful worth!

So soar high, dear heart, in the sky,
With dreams on the wings where the wild ones lie.
Each flap is a giggle, each glide a toast,
To the whimsy of life, let's all raise a boast!

Sprouts of Resilience

In the garden of dreams, we try to grow,
With sun hats on tight, we steal the show.
Watering worries with laughter and cheer,
Watch the weeds dance; no need to sneer.

Beneath the compost, some secrets reside,
Worms have their parties, but they won't collide.
We cheer for the sprouts, green and so spry,
Who knew roots could boogie beneath the sky?

Our leafy friends twirl in the summer breeze,
They wear little capes, oh what a tease!
With each funny wilt, they holler and joke,
In the patch of delight, they giggle and poke.

So when life gets tough, just look to the ground,
With each quirky sprout, new laughter is found.
Plant seeds of your dreams and see what they'll do,
For joy is a garden, and you'll see it too!

A Symphony of New Beginnings

A toe-tapping tune from the buds on the vine,
With blossoms a-glimmer, and sunshine divine.
The daisies are humming, the tulips can jive,
In this floral fest, oh, how we thrive!

A kite in the sky takes flight with a twist,
While daisies debate if they should coexist.
The roses roll laughter, the lilies make gaffes,
In this orchestra, we all share the laughs.

New shoots burst forth with a shimmy and shake,
While garden gnomes dance, make no mistake.
Each bud has a story, some silly and grand,
With petals for pages, they make their stand.

So join in the chorus, come sing with delight,
For every new blossom brings joy to the sight.
In this symphony bright, let your spirit take wing,
And dance with the flowers, it's a magical fling!

The Bloom of Tomorrow's Light

In a pot on the sill, a sunflower bleats,
With dreams of the sky and some whimsical beats.
It stretches its leaves, fluffed up with glee,
Whispering secrets to the busy bumblebee.

With petals that giggle in rays of gold,
It brags of the stories that never get old.
A crocus pops up like, "Look at me thrive!"
With a wink and a nod, it's truly alive!

Oh, the garden's alive with shenanigans bright,
As tulips wear sunglasses to soak up the light.
While daisies debate on the best way to pose,
For a snapshot that captures their bloom as it grows.

Embrace every sprout as they spread their charms,
In this dance of the flora with all of its balms.
When life feels too heavy, just gaze at the sight,
Of blooms sharing laughter, igniting the night!

Journey to Abundant Skies

In the expedition of plants, there's a whimsical cheer,
With carrots in uniforms, all lining up near.
Each veggie a traveler, with stories to tell,
Of storms they've endured and how they grew well.

Pumpkins rolling onward, proud in their bulk,
Golfing in grass till the time for their hulk.
While peas in their pods have a gossip along,
Trading their tales in a vegetable song.

From sprouts on a mission to flowers in flight,
Each leaf joins the quest, oh what a sight!
They dream of the sun and the clouds up above,
Throwing their seeds like confetti of love.

Together they wander beneath skies so vast,
With laughter in clusters, they leave their past.
In the journey of green as they march ever high,
They whisper of hope in a natural sky!

Garden Grown in Faith

In the garden where we jest,
We water dreams, we plant the best.
We coax the weeds, give them a chat,
While daisies giggle; how about that?

Tomatoes dance and peppers sway,
As we mulch nonsense in the clay.
We sing to sprouts, and the sun complies,
With joy so bright, it blinds our eyes.

A harvest feast, all laughter and cheer,
Pickled cucumbers and some good beer.
With every bite, a story's shared,
Of hope's sweet bloom, of love declared.

So plant your seeds, take a chance,
In every garden, give laughter a dance.
For faith is wild, like weeds gone high,
Amidst the giggles, we reach for the sky.

Echoes of Future Light

Whispers of laughter bounce in the air,
Like jazz bands playing without a care.
We wander paths where dreams collide,
With silly faces, we take a ride.

Each step we take, a mistake so grand,
Yet in our hearts, we understand.
The echoes of giggles ring out so clear,
As hope's bright glow draws ever near.

A tapestry woven with threads of cheer,
Creating stories we hold so dear.
A future painted in vibrant hues,
With every giggle, we'll never lose.

So catch those rays, let your heart ignite,
In the symphony of the coming light.
For every chuckle is a seed we sow,
Together in laughter, we all will grow.

The Sweetest Yield

With cupcakes swirling, dreams take flight,
In kitchens where we bake with delight.
Flavor explosions, giggles, and fluff,
Like marshmallow clouds, isn't it tough?

Silly recipes written in haste,
With laughter mixed in, oh, what a taste!
Chocolate fountains that splash and glow,
Running amok, oh, don't be so slow!

Candied hopes lie on a dish,
Each frosting swirl, a silly wish.
We harvest smiles, both big and small,
In the sweetest yield, we embrace them all.

So let's indulge in this joyous spree,
With every bite, a chance to be free.
For in each laugh and mirthful cheer,
We find the sweetness that draws us near.

Horizon's Embrace

On the edge of the day, we squint and stare,
Finding funny shapes in the evening air.
The sun bows low, with a wink and a grin,
As we chase shadows of laughter in.

Clouds doing cartwheels across the blue,
Tickling the stars with a cosmic view.
A horizon painted with colors galore,
We laugh together, always wanting more.

Chasing dreams like butterflies bright,
Envisioning futures wrapped in delight.
With every giggle, the world can sway,
In the embrace of joy, we dance all day.

So let's paint our tomorrows with cheer,
Daring the sun to shine even near.
For in every laugh, the world turns new,
And hope's embrace is waiting for you.

Gentle Yet Strong

Breezes dance through trees, quite spry,
They tickle leaves and make them sigh.
A snail wears shades and sunblock too,
Saying, "I'll move fast, just watch me do!"

Clouds float by with playful grins,
Whispering secrets of tiny wins.
A squirrel with snacks starts a parade,
Chasing the shadows that laughter made.

When flowers bloom in colors bright,
They giggle under the soft moonlight.
A toad in a top hat sings a tune,
While fireflies twirl like stars in June.

So here's a toast, with roots and cheer,
To all the laughter we hold dear.
For strength and giggles go hand in hand,
In this quirky, wacky, wonderful land.

Wading Through Light

In puddles of sunshine, I frolic and play,
Splashing through giggles, come join the ballet!
The shadows throw parties, inviting the sun,
While ants hold a meeting on who's the most fun.

Bouncing through daisies, blooms poke my toes,
The wind whispers jokes that only it knows.
I twirl and I whirl, feeling quite free,
As butterflies chuckle and dance around me.

With raindrops like diamonds, I gather a few,
To trade for a treasure – a spritz of bright dew.
The sun sings a tune as I wade through the light,
Putting smiles on faces with joy that's just right.

So join in the fun, let's splash and let's sway,
Life's a whimsical dance, come wade in today!
For in this bright world, with laughter we mingle,
A splash here and there makes our hearts feel a jingle.

Sowing Circles of Joy

With pockets of seeds, we'll plant our delight,
Sprouting wild giggles that tickle the night.
A garden of chuckles, where silly rains fall,
And daisies wear hats that are way too tall.

A bumblebee buzzes with a pun on its lips,
While grasshoppers cartwheel with flips and with drips.
"Let's grow us a tickle, a snicker, a cheer,
For laughter's the sunlight that keeps us all near!"

So scatter the bubbles, let joy take its flight,
As we dance with the daisies, so merry and bright.
Each bloom is a smile, each leaf spins a tale,
In this garden of fun, where we never turn pale.

So let's sow these circles, with laughter and glee,
A field of enchantment for you and for me.
With every seed planted, a giggle will grow,
In the heart of this laughter, together we'll glow.

Dreams on the Wind

As dreams ride the breeze like a mischievous kite,
They tickle the clouds and giggle in flight.
A cat in a hat makes a wish on a star,
While llamas in pajamas say, "Look at us far!"

The whispers of wishes swirl round and round,
On paths made of jellybeans, dreams can be found.
With giggles like bubbles and sparkles so bold,
Let's chase 'em with laughter, their magic unfolds.

So let's hop on a cloud, wear feathers galore,
With unicorns dancing, who could ask for more?
With dreams on the wind and laughter in tow,
Life's a carnival ride that's ready to go!

So let's spin our wishes and dive into fun,
For dreaming together's the best little run.
With joy as our compass, we'll soar and we'll sing,
On this wild, whimsical, magical wing.

Promises in the Breeze

A squirrel danced, tail in a swirl,
Chasing dreams in a hazel whirl.
Leaves giggled as they twirled around,
Nature's whispers, a joyful sound.

Pies in windows, scents that tease,
Lemonade stands set up with ease.
Lemon drops and laughter flow,
Sunshine bright, all worries go.

Clouds above, like marshmallows float,
A paper boat on a giggly moat.
With each gust, the world feels light,
Even weeds can sparkle bright.

So let's toast with a berry cheer,
To everyone who joins us here.
Life is fun, let's live it bold,
In every moment, warmth untold.

When Wishes Take Wing

A paper crane filled with dreams,
Floats above on sunny beams.
It flaps and flutters, seeking flight,
A giggle here, a wink of light.

Balloons rise with laughter loud,
Dance with joy, draw in a crowd.
Each wish whispers as they soar,
Beneath our feet, imagination's floor.

What if shirts could magically clean?
And socks could sing like a wobbly queen?
With every wish, the world feels strange,
But isn't that just part of change?

So let's chase those dreams we hold,
With open hearts and spirits bold.
When wishes take wing, let us see,
How funny life can truly be.

Everlasting Light

A twinkling star forgot to sleep,
In skies that giggle and brightly peep.
Nighttime chuckles, it draws near,
A firefly winks: 'Don't shed a tear!'

Glow sticks dance in vibrant glee,
As shadows join in, just wait and see.
Each burst of light, a playful fight,
Why can't shadows have some delight?

Candles lean in, share a joke,
As laughter flows and silence broke.
In every flicker, joy ignites,
Finding warmth in starry nights.

So gather round, let laughter shine,
In every dark, there's a silver line.
Everlasting glow, not just for show,
In every heart, it starts to grow.

The Symphony of Growth

In a garden where laughter seeds,
Green beans giggle, sprouting needs.
Onions chuckle, in cozy rows,
Each plant plays where the sunshine glows.

Butterflies dance on twinkling tunes,
While daisies sway with playful prunes.
Rain taps gently, a joyful beat,
As roots wiggle in the warm retreat.

Frogs croak out their silly song,
Toads jump in, they all belong.
Nature's orchestra, loud and proud,
Makes every heart feel freely wowed.

So let the sprouts and blooms inspire,
With every note, we'll rise higher.
In this rhythm, let's grow anew,
Life's a concert, just for you!

Winged Aspirations

In the park, a pigeon struts,
With dreams of crumbs in buttered huts.
He coos, he flares, a side-eye glance,
Thinks he's part of a food ballet dance.

A kid with chips, he makes a lunge,
The pigeon pops, performs a plunge.
He flaps his wings, as if to say,
"One day, I'll fly far away!"

The trees above, they shake with glee,
As squirrels plot their own mystery.
With nuts in hand, they laugh and cheer,
Chasing dreams, no hint of fear.

So watch and wonder as they play,
In this silly world, they'll find their way!
For even pigeons dream of bread,
While squirrels build paths to the skies ahead.

A Canvas of Dreams

In a corner of the art-filled room,
A toddler paints the walls with groom.
With colors splashed, and a joyful cheer,
Mom hopes it's not permanent here!

The brush strokes wild, like a puppy's tail,
She giggles loud, a bright detail.
Each splotch a plan to paint the sun,
Surely, with laughter, we'll call it fun!

Doodles dance around like bees,
With crayon dresses, and chalk-swirled trees.
To her, each mess is a treasure found,
Her masterpiece sprawls all around.

In colors bright and swirls galore,
Who needs a gallery? Let's paint some more!
For in this chaos, joy is born,
The heart's wide canvas, forever adorned.

Fruits of the Heart

In the garden, fruits grow bold,
With tales of sweetness yet untold.
A grape once dreamed, of wine and cheer,
But settled for juice, less severe!

An orange peeked from leafy greens,
Said, "I'd rather be in tasty scenes!"
So citrus squished with delight and sound,
While lemons joined—oh what a round!

Bananas laughed, with a monkey's swing,
Said, "Life is better when we sing!"
With peels all bright, they danced in rows,
Whispering laughs, as the garden grows.

So pick a fruit, savor the whim,
In this fruity life, we'll never dim!
For in the garden, grinning wide,
The heart grows sweeter, side by side.

Lighthouses in the Storm

The lighthouse flickers, a cheeky grin,
Winking at waves, as the storm rolls in.
"Bring it on!" it shouts with glee,
"I've got bulbs for days and snacks for sea!"

Seagulls squawk, circling round,
"Hey lighthouse! You wear the crown!"
As thunder rumbles with boisterous cheer,
They swoop and dive, with nothing to fear.

The waves crash high, like a game of tags,
While the lighthouse laughs, shaking its flags.
In this chaos, a dance unfolds,
Twisting twirls of brave and bold.

Through squall and gale, the beacon beams,
In every heart, where laughter streams.
Lighthouses stand, in stormy play,
Guiding us home, come what may!

www.ingramcontent.com/pod-product-compliance
Lightning Source LLC
Chambersburg PA
CBHW070321120526
44590CB00017B/2777